The Puppy Baby Book

by Dawn Greenfield Ireland

illustrated and designed by Gladys Ramirez
edited by M.A.S. Stautberg

ARTISTIC ORIGINS

Published in the United States by Artistic Origins Publications
A Division of Artistic Origins, P. O. Box 584, Bellaire, TX 77401
www.artistic-origins.com

Kaopectate® is a trademark of Pharmacia and Upjohn Consumer Healthcare
Dramamine® is a trademark of Pharmacia and Upjohn Consumer Healthcare
Disclaimer — consult your pet's veterinarian before administering any medications.

04 03 02 01 00   9 8 7 6 5 4 3 2 1

ISBN No. 0-9701137-0-6

illustrated and designed by Gladys Ramirez

edited by M.A.S. Stautberg

logo design by Linda Bajumpaa

project management by Rita Mills / Mills & Morris Publishing, Inc.

ARTISTIC ORIGINS

For Brandon, George and Shasta

In memory of George and Dorothy Greenfield,
and my best friend, Joseph Charles Feduccia

Dog

There is no mistake in the spelling of dog

For God in heaven knows those four paws

That furry face and wagging tail

Ears perked up

Waiting to sail

Across the clouds at His side

Romping, barking the Kingdom-wide

Dancing with angels every day

God's best friend is but a lick away

A Note from the Author

Congratulations on adopting your beautiful puppy. As you journey through your puppy's first year you will make many discoveries about your new charge, and yourself. Dogs offer such unconditional love and ask for so little in return.

A pat on the head, brushing their coat, a walk in any type of weather, or a ride in the car brings incredible joy to our best friends. As you get to know your puppy you will discover his / her personality as it blooms. Some dogs are happy-go-lucky, like my little girl Shasta. Others are worriers, scaredy-cats, mischief-makers, or manipulators.

It distresses me when I hear of a dog that is chained or plunked out in a back yard with little companionship. That is not much of an existence. Dogs are very social creatures and require love and affection. They suffer in isolation. Excessive barking is one way a dog communicates that he is bored, lonely, or frightened. Destructive behavior is another way that dogs try to let you know there is something amiss. Pay attention to your dog and you will have the best friend in the world.

I urge you to become involved in your dog's life and to consider joining some of the marvelous animal welfare organizations that strive for quality animal lives. A sampling of these organizations are listed in the back of this book.

If after perusing these pages you discover situations that you wish had been included, please send me an email (author@artistic-origins.com) or write to the publisher. I would like to have your input for the next printing.

Thank you for purchasing The Puppy Baby Book.

author@artistic-origins.com

Look for other titles in this series: The Kitten Baby Book, My New Home (for older dogs and cats), The Birdie Baby Book, and In Memory Of

www.artistic-origins.com

The Puppy Baby Book

My Baby Picture

My Birth

"All of the animals except man know that the principal business of life is to enjoy it." Anonymous

I was born on .... , ... at .... ☐ a.m. ☐ p.m.

in .... , ...
(City) (State) (Country)

My mother's name is ....

Her breed is ....

Her guardians are ....

My father's name is ....

His breed is ....

His guardians are ....

My guardians named me ....

Tip: Puppies are curious. Make sure you do not keep medications, poisons, mousetraps, glue traps, or even chocolate within their reach.

Dog Family Pictures

My Mom

My Dad

My Paw Prints

Tip: Use a non-toxic ink or paint to make your puppy paw prints, Be sure to wash your puppy's feet before you let him down on the floor!

Litter Pictures

My Litter

There were .... of us in my litter. Of .... brothers and .... sisters, I was born number .... My guardians said I was a .... (Healthy/sickly/strong/weak) puppy and I resemble my ❑ mom ❑ dad.

My fur is .... Long, short, curly, straight and .... Color . My eyes are ....

You could tell me apart from my littermates because I was the ❑ brave ❑ whining ❑ curious ❑ hungry one who had the ❑ funny ❑ timid ❑ outgoing ❑ winning personality. Plus, I had special ❑ coloration ❑ markings on my ❑ face ❑ neck ❑ tummy ❑ back ❑ ears ❑ tail.

I ❑ nursed ❑ was bottle fed with .... and I was weaned on .... , My first meal after weaning was .... and my first puppy food was ....

Tip: Dogs **MUST** have access to water 24-hours a day. Use a heavy ceramic bowl to prevent tipping accidents. Consider elevating food and water bowls to prevent neck strain.

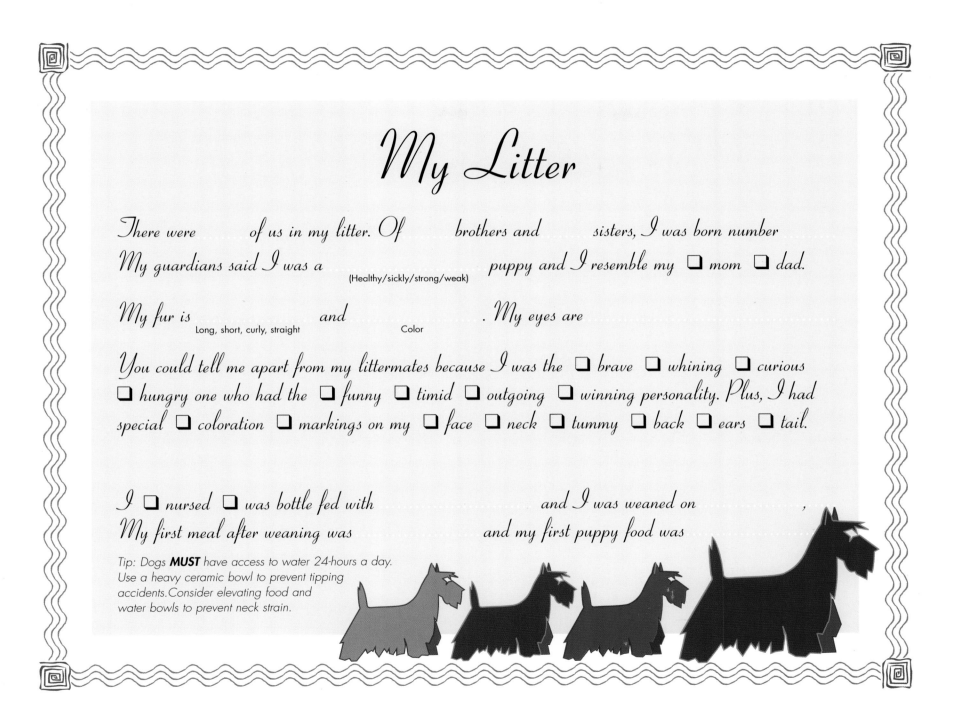

More Picture-Perfect Moments

My Adoption

On _____ , _____ , when I was _____ old, I was adopted by _____

of _____
(Complete address)

I ☐ missed ☐ did not miss my mother and siblings. I cried for _____ ☐ days ☐ nights ☐ weeks.

My new name is _____

And my nickname is _____

The folks also call me _____ and _____

Tip: Puppies need a warm, snuggly place to sleep, such as a box or bed containing a piece of fleece or a warm rug.

My Adoption Papers

My Adoption Announcement

See the webpage to order adoption announcement cards. www.artistic-origins.com

My Credentials

My Identity

I am a VIP
(very important puppy)
because I am a full blooded

(Mutt, Beagle, etc.)

My New Family

My New Family

I know my new mommy as .... and ....
                                           (Mommy, etc.)   (Actual name)

My new daddy's name is .... and ....
                                           (Daddy, etc.)   (Actual name)

I have .... grandmas and .... grandpas. Their names are ....

....

....

My aunts and uncles are ....

....

....

....

Home

Tip: Make sure that you keep a close eye on your puppy when he goes outside. Do not let him eat anything on the ground. Ant baits and other pesticides are poisonous, and are easily forgotten dangers. Do not let your puppy walk on grass that has been recently sprayed for fleas until the grass is completely dry.

Playmates

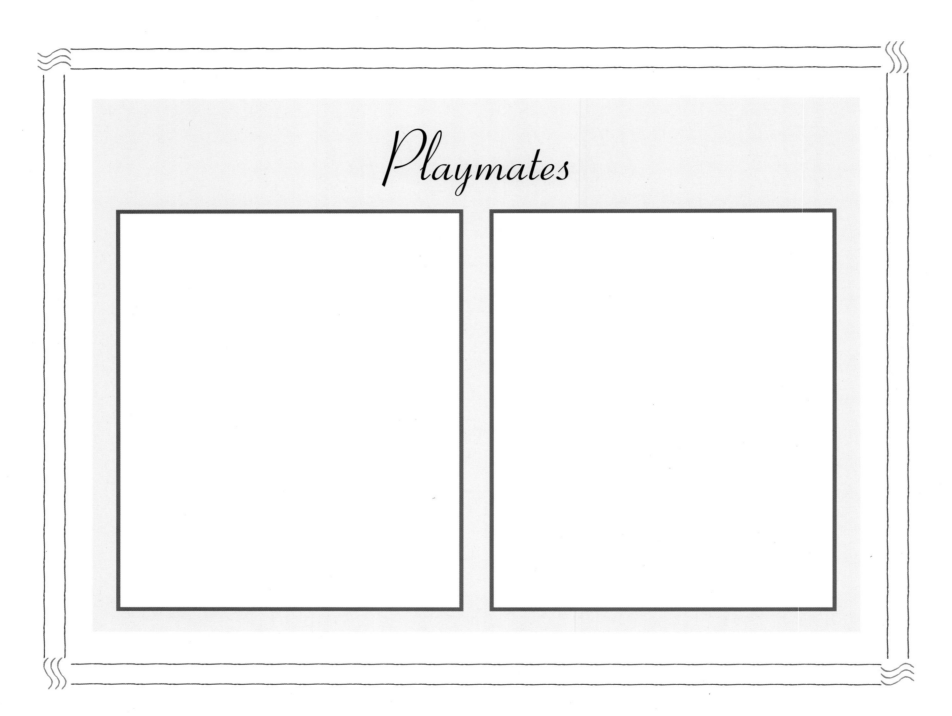

Human Playmates

My human playmates are ....
(Children's names)

....

....

....

I sleep with: .... ❑ on a ❑ the ❑ in a
(Human, animal, toy)

On ...., ... I had my first bath. ❑ I liked ❑ did not like that experience.

I began potty training when I was .... old and accomplished complete

comprehension of what was expected of me ❑ after ❑ in just

❑ hours ❑ days ❑ weeks ❑ months, by .... ,

Tip: Paper the town, or at least the floor, until your puppy is housebroken. Accidents happen. When a mistake occurs, clean up the mess immediately and thoroughly. If a puppy smells a spot where he has relieved himself, he is more than likely going to use that spot again. DO NOT rub your puppy's nose in his mess if he makes a mistake. Instead, bring it to his attention where he is supposed to relieve himself. Potty training takes time.

Graduation Picture

Obedience School

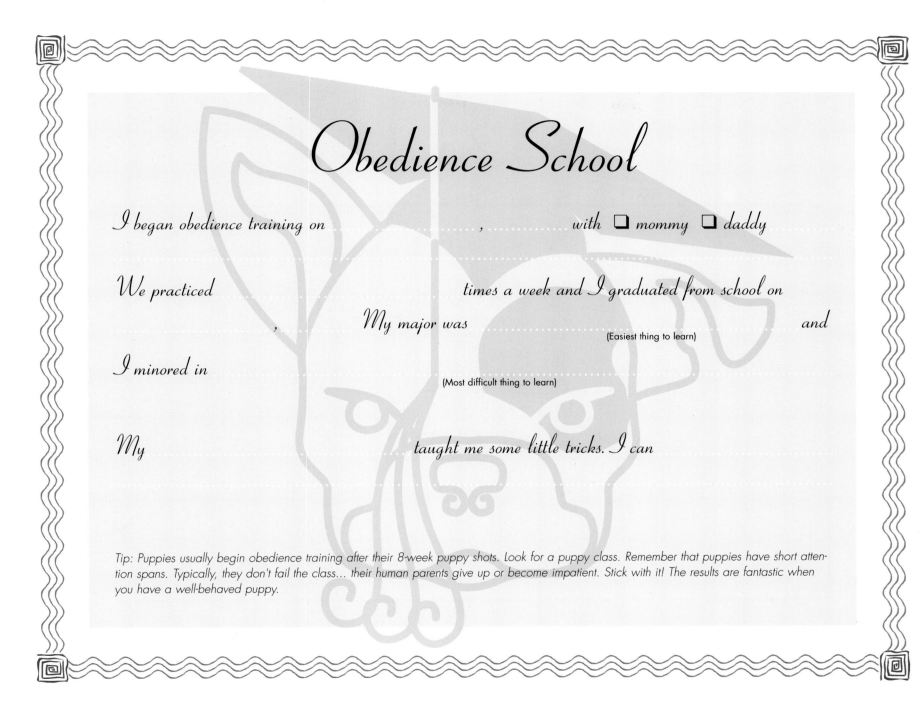

I began obedience training on _____ , _____ with ☐ mommy ☐ daddy

We practiced _____ times a week and I graduated from school on

_____ , My major was _____ and

(Easiest thing to learn)

I minored in _____

(Most difficult thing to learn)

My _____ taught me some little tricks. I can

Tip: Puppies usually begin obedience training after their 8-week puppy shots. Look for a puppy class. Remember that puppies have short attention spans. Typically, they don't fail the class... their human parents give up or become impatient. Stick with it! The results are fantastic when you have a well-behaved puppy.

Pals

My New Friend

I have a new friend. ☐ His ☐ her name is ....

And ☐ he ☐ she is a ....
(Dog, cat, pig, bird, hamster, etc.)

We met on .... , ... at ....

I liked ☐ him ☐ her ☐ right away ☐ it took me a little while to get used to ☐ him ☐ her.

My other friends are ....

Things I do with my friends are ....

....

"[Dogs] are better than human beings, because they know but do not tell." Emily Dickinson, American poet (1830-1886)

19

Here I Am Again

Tidbits of Information about Me

I am afraid of

(Loud noises, thunder, babies, cars, etc.)

My favorite things to do are:

Run and play in the ☐ yard ☐ park

Go to the ☐ ocean ☐ lake

Romp through ☐ puddles ☐ snow ☐ leaves

Chase ☐ squirrels ☐ butterflies

Chew on my chew toys

Ride in the ☐ car ☐ truck ☐ boat ☐ plane ☐ bike

Go to _____ house.

I take my vitamins every day. I take

My favorite snacks are

Places I like to nap are

My favorite toy is

My wardrobe consists of

(Leash, collar, harness, sweaters, coats, rain gear, bandana)

Fact: Dogs have 319 bones, the same in all breeds and all sizes. People have 204 bones, cats 244. Adult dogs have 42 teeth and puppies have 28 teeth.

Good Dog

Bad Dog

The Clinic

Here's the place

The Staff

My Doctor

My veterinarian is

Dr. ....

at ....

(Name of clinic)

My Veterinarian

My First Rabies Tag

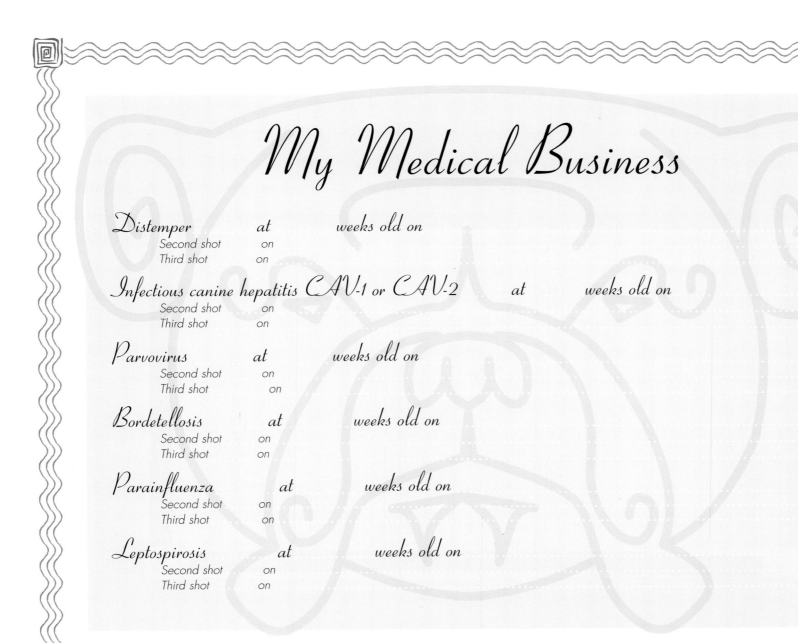

My Medical Business

Distemper   at   weeks old on
Second shot   on
Third shot   on

Infectious canine hepatitis CAV-1 or CAV-2   at   weeks old on
Second shot   on
Third shot   on

Parvovirus   at   weeks old on
Second shot   on
Third shot   on

Bordetellosis   at   weeks old on
Second shot   on
Third shot   on

Parainfluenza   at   weeks old on
Second shot   on
Third shot   on

Leptospirosis   at   weeks old on
Second shot   on
Third shot   on

Important Medical Papers

More Medical Business

Rabies   at   weeks old on
    Second shot   on
    Third shot   on

Coronavirus   at   weeks old on
    Second shot   on
    Third shot   on

Lyme Disease   at   weeks old on
    Second shot   on
    Third shot   on

Kennel Cough   at   weeks old on
    Second shot   on
    Third shot   on

❑ *Spay*   ❑ *Neuter*   on
    By

(Veterinarian or clinic name & address)

Tip: Have your puppy tattooed or have a microchip identification chip implanted. If your puppy becomes lost and loses his collar, he will be able to be identified and returned to you safely. See page 71 for information on the AKC Companion Animal Retrieval System.

See My Boo-Boo's

My Medical Business *Continued*

De-wormed (How embarrassing!) .... at .... weeks old on ....

Fecal Exam .... at .... weeks old on ....

Heartworm test .... at .... weeks old on ....

My Medical Emergencies and Blunders

Getting Bigger Everyday

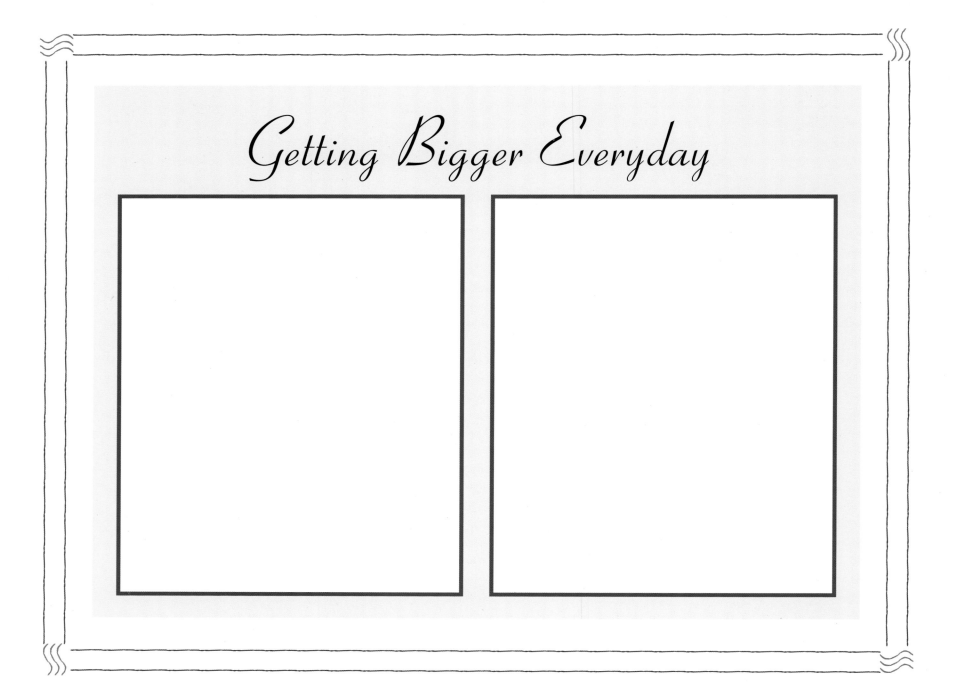

See How Big I Am!

Birth weight .... lbs. .... oz. Height from shoulders .... rump ....

6 weeks .... lbs. .... oz. Height from shoulders .... rump ....

6 months .... lbs. .... oz. Height from shoulders .... rump ....

1 year .... lbs. .... oz. Height from shoulders .... rump ....

18 months .... lbs. .... oz. Height from shoulders .... rump ....

2 years .... lbs. .... oz. Height from shoulders .... rump ....

Taking Medicine

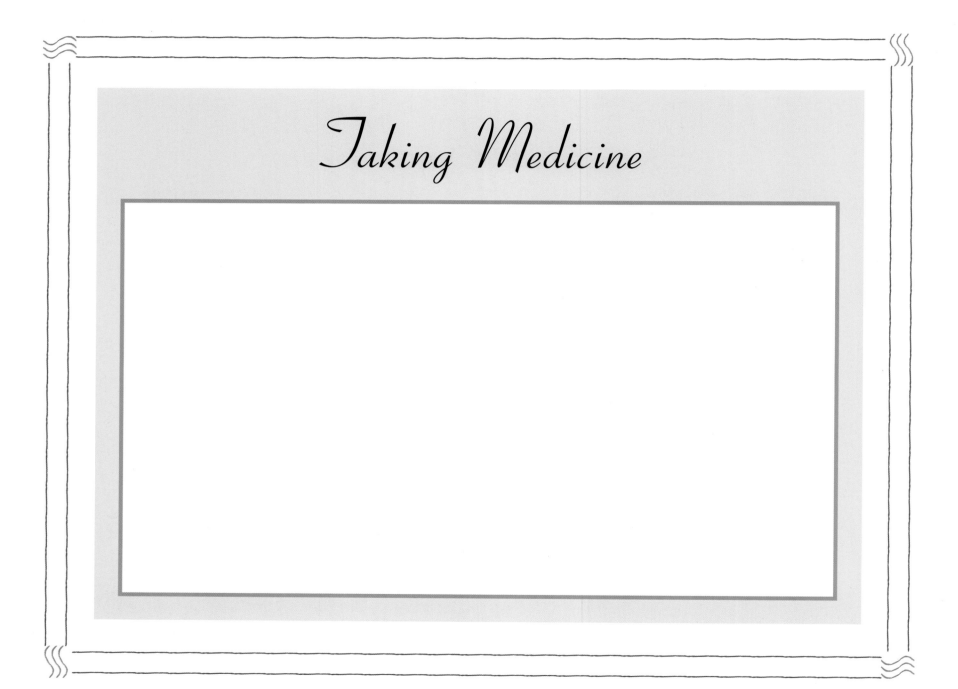

First Aid Kit

Emergencies happen and it is best to be prepared. Keep the following items on hand in your pet first aid kit:

Gauze rolls or pads
Adhesive tape
Cotton
Scissors, rounded tip and pointed
Hydrogen peroxide
Antibiotic ointment
Hydrocortisone cream
Eyewash
Tweezers
Rectal thermometer
Oral medication syringe
Antihistamine liquid
Baby aspirin - buffered aspirin only
Kaopectate®(One teaspoon for each 10 pounds of weight.)
Bismuth (One teaspoon for each 20 pounds of weight, every four to six hours. DO NOT give to cats.)
Dramamine®(For small dogs, give 12.5 milligrams. Medium to large dogs, give 20 to 50 milligrams one hour before travelling.)

WARNING: Do not use acetaminophen or ibuprofen. Both are dangerous for pets.
WARNING: Consult your pet's veterinarian before administrating any medications.

Happy Birthday To Me

My First Birthday

This is how we marked my special day

Me and Mommy

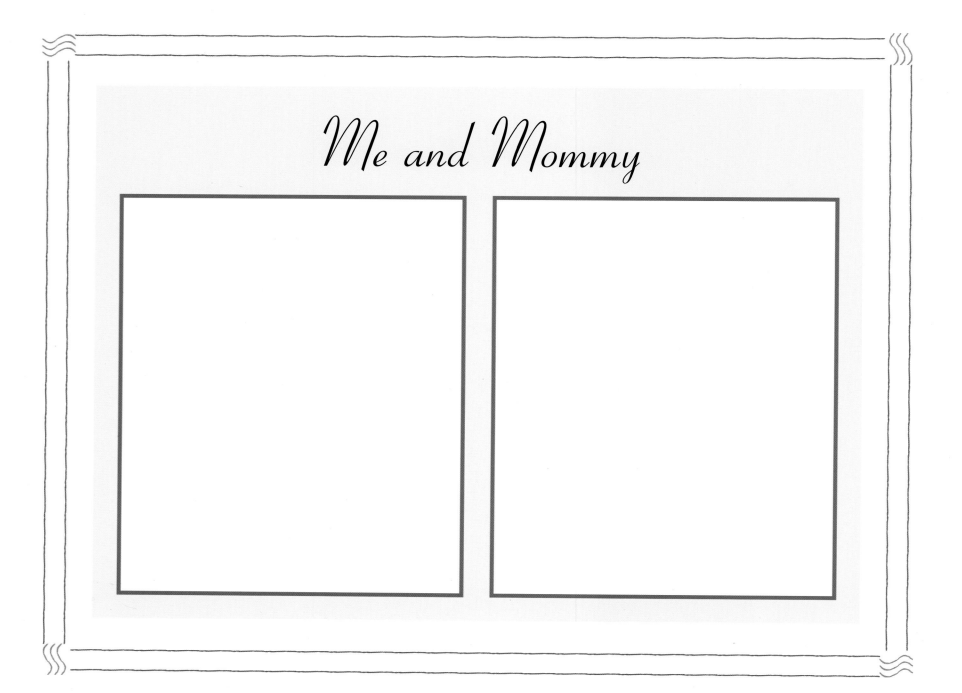

Mommy's Birthday

Me and Daddy

Daddy's Birthday

Chinese New Year

A day of good fortune.

New Year's Day

Valentine's Day

Be mine.

Mardi Gras

St. Patrick's Day

April Fool's Day

Good Friday

I gave up fleas for Lent.

Easter Sunday

Me and Mommy

Mother's Day

Holiday Fun

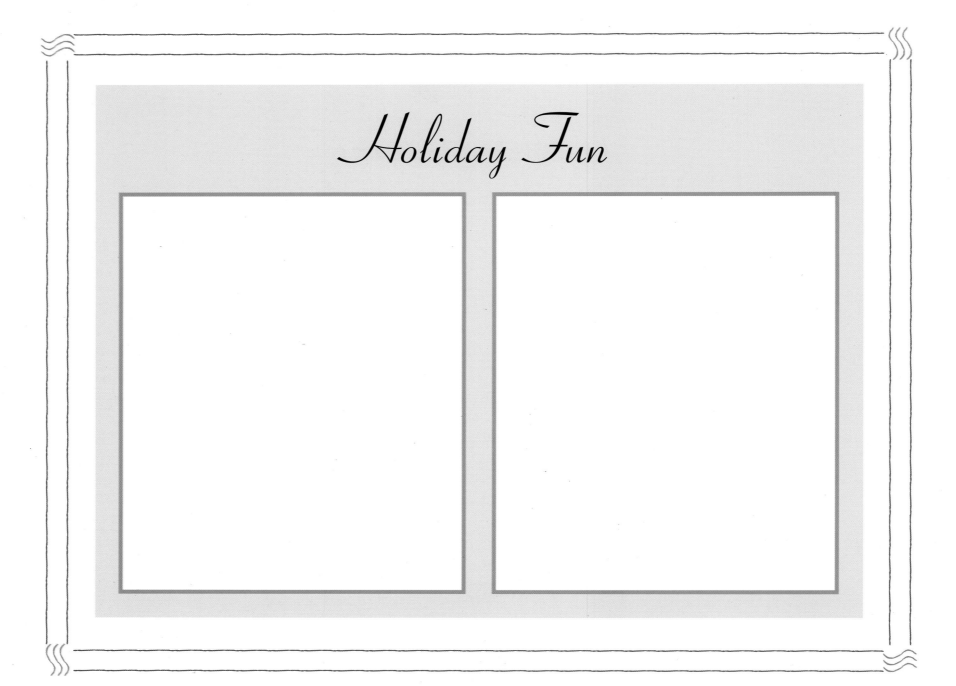

Memorial Day

Me and Daddy

Father's Day

Independence Day

Keep me away from those firecrackers!

Labor Day

One Happy Family

Grandparent's Day

Rosh Hashanah

Yom Kippur

Trick or Treat

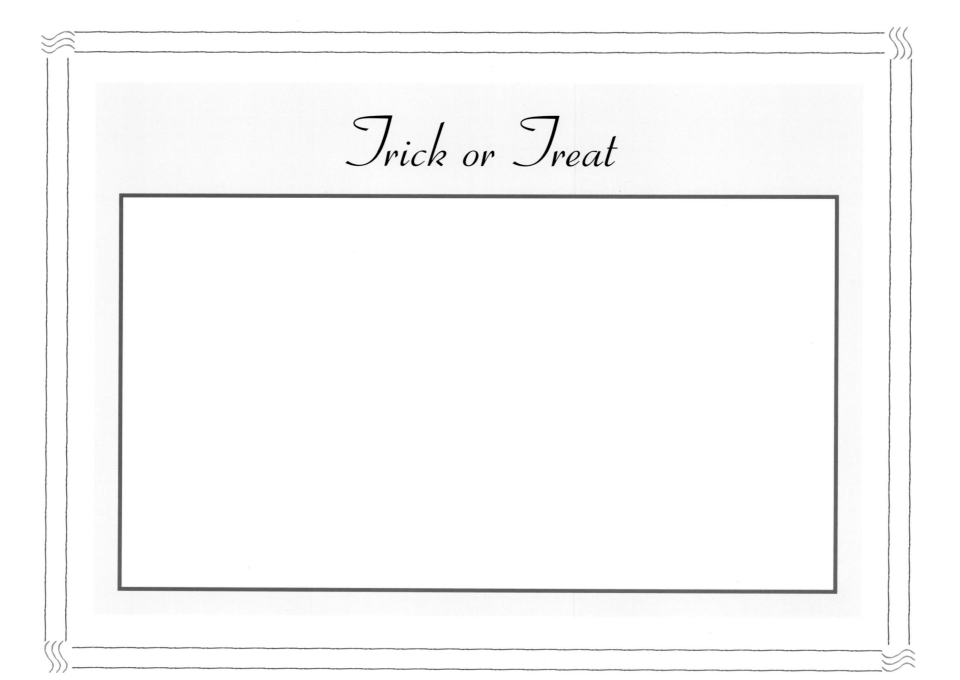

Halloween

A Day of Thanks

Thanksgiving Day

Hanukkah

Christmas

Fun, Fun, Fun

Other Special Days

Animal Organizations

American Society for the Prevention of Cruelty to Animals (ASPCA)
424 East 92nd St.
New York, NY 10128
www.aspca.org

Animal Legal Defense Fund
127 Fourth St.
Petaluma, CA 94952
800-555-6517
action@aldf.org
www.aldf.org

Best Friends Animal Sanctuary
Kanab, Utah 84741
435-644-2001
info@bestfriends.org
www.bestfriends.org

People for the Ethical Treatment of Animals (PETA)
501 Front St.,
Norfolk, VA 23510
757-622-PETA
info@peta-online.org
www.peta.com

Doris Day Animal League
227 Massachusetts Ave. NE #100
Washington DC 20002
202-546-1761
www.ddal.org

Last Chance for Animals
8033 sunset Blvd. #35
Los Angeles, CA 90046
310-271-6096
fax 310-271-1890
www.lcanimals.org

More Animal Organizations

PCRM

5100 Wisconson Ave. NW #404
Washington DC 20016
202-686-2210
Fax 202-686-2216
www.pcrm.org

**Association of
Veterinarians
for Animal Rights**

P. O. Box 208
Davis, CA 95617-0208
530-759-8166
Fax 530-759-8116
www.avar.org
avar@agc.org

**Animal Rights
Resource Site**

www.animalconcerns.org

**AKC Companion Animal
Recovery/Home Again
Companion Animal
Retrieval System**

5580 Centerview Dr.,
Suite 250
Raleigh, NC 27606-3394
800-252-7894
found@akc.org
www.akc.org/car.htm

**The Humane Society of
the United States (HSUS)**

2100 L. Street, NW
Washington DC 20037
202-452-1100
Fax: 301-548-7700
www.hsus.org<http://www.hsus.org>

Order Form

Corporations/Organizations, Kennel Clubs and Veterinarians call 832-687-3194

Title	Qty.	Price	Total
The Puppy Baby Book		$21.95	
Adoption Announcement Cards (8)		$3.50	
Adoption Certificate		$4.99	
Authentic Credentials Certificate		$4.99	
Puppy Adoption Kit (includes all of the above)		$32.00	

☐ VISA ☐ MC ☐ AMEX ☐ DISCOVER

Cardholder Name _____

Card Number _____ Expiration _____

Signature _____

Subtotal _____

TX Residents Add 8.25% tax _____

Shipping _____

($4 for first book, $2 for each additional book, $5 for each Puppy Adobption Kit, $0.85 for each certificate, $1.21 for each card set)

TOTAL ENCLOSED _____

Ship to:
Name _____
Address _____
City/State/Zip _____
Daytime Phone _____
Email _____

Order online at www.artistic-origins.com

Check or Money Order to:

Artistic Origins
P.O. Box 584
Bellaire, TX 77402

Canada & Foreign:

Sent Airmail. Credit Card orders only. Canada: Multiply U.S. shipping X4. Foreign: Multiply U.S. shipping X8.

U.S. Orders:

Sent USPS Ground. Allow 7-10 business days. Please enclose proper tax and shipping.

Fax Your Orders to:

713-355-8614